Malahide at the Millennium

MALAHIDE CAMERA CLUB

ISBN – 0 9538374 0 8

Designed by Artwerk

Printed by ColourBooks Ltd.

INTRODUCTION

As we embark upon a new millennium, this book sets out to capture a moment in time in the lives of the people of Malahide. We reflect upon the cultural heritage, the present occupations and the future aspirations of this lively and diverse community.

From the very beginning, the area around Malahide was an attractive place to live and there is evidence to suggest it was one of the earliest settled areas in Ireland. Artefacts from the Mesolithic era have been unearthed from Paddy's hill, a hill that later in 432 A.D. St. Patrick reputedly visited. In 795 A.D. the Vikings arrived and were later followed by the Normans.

In 1184 Sir Richard de Talbot was granted the Lordship of Malahide and for almost 800 years (apart from a brief period in the Cromwellian era) the Talbot family have resided at Malahide Castle. The Talbot – Malahide connection finally ended in 1976 when the Castle and Demesne were bought by Dublin County Council.

Today Malahide is a flourishing residential and tourist town with a population of about 20,000. The sporting facilities are numerous and diverse and there is also a wealth of interest for the botanist, ornithologist, historian, artist and archaeologist. The photographs in this book focus on the various activities of a closely-knit community at work, at rest and at play – a community which takes pride not only in preserving its rich heritage but also in enriching it for the future generations.

The Editorial Team: Harry Reynolds, Deirdre Gaffney, Colm Reilly and Mervyn Robinson. – **7**

This book was made possible by the generous assistance of:

————————

Mr. Michael Howard,
"Michael Howard and Associates"

————————

Ms. Aideen Murphy,
"The Medical Hall",

————————

Mr. John Duffy,
"Duffy's Pub",

————————

Dr. John and Mrs. Elizabeth Kirker,
"The Casino",

————————

Mr. Tony Gibney,
"Gibney's Pub"

————————

Mr. Eric Crampton,
"The Pottery Shop",

————————

Mr. Tony Byrne,
"Tony Byrne's Menswear",

————————

Mr. Noel Smyth,
"Smyth's Pub",

————————

Ms. Karen Kirby,
A.I.B. Bank,

————————

Mr. Al Ryan,
"The Grand Hotel"

And

The National Millennium Committee.

Early morning on the estuary. – 6

Michael Durkin prepares for another day's work. His garden centre has been located at the Diamond for 15 years. **– 14**

The Carnegie Library was built in 1909 from Portmarnock Brick at a cost of £1000. The first librarian was Mr. Clery. — **20**

Killeen Terrace was built on the former site of McIntyre's Silk Factory by John Killeen as a dowry for his daughter. However, she entered a convent and shattered his plans. — **20**

A single footprint of an early morning stroller. – **15**

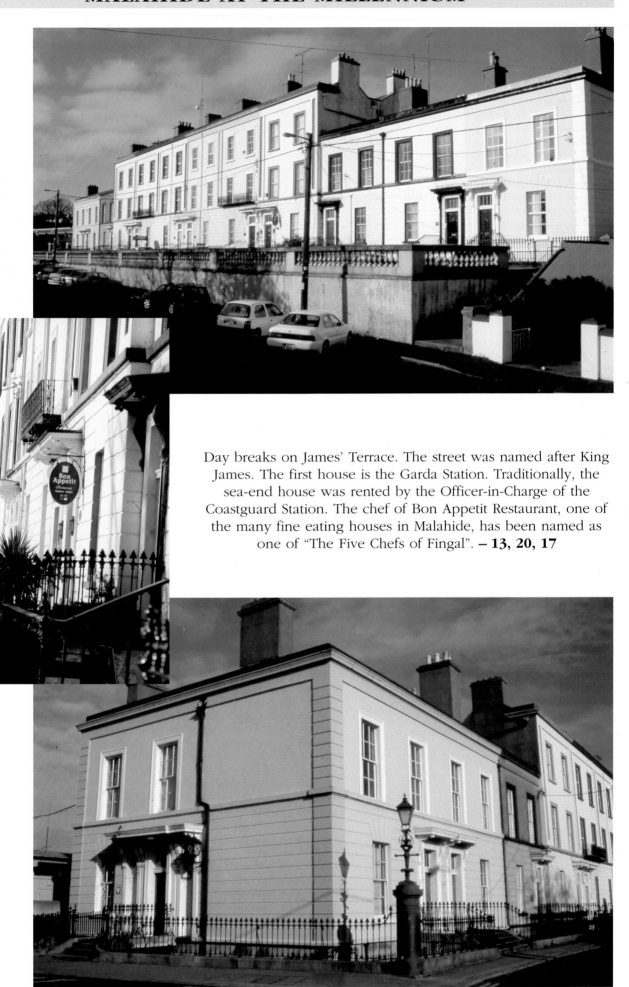

Day breaks on James' Terrace. The street was named after King James. The first house is the Garda Station. Traditionally, the sea-end house was rented by the Officer-in-Charge of the Coastguard Station. The chef of Bon Appetit Restaurant, one of the many fine eating houses in Malahide, has been named as one of "The Five Chefs of Fingal". – **13, 20, 17**

Postperson, Denny Keenan. — **7**

Colin Maher, faithful attendant at McAllister's Garage and friend to all. — **2**

Frank Timmons and friend. — **17**

90 year-old Sara Forde, taking her morning stroll in Malahide Garden Centre. — **17**

Two French children on the beach. — **10**

David Kinna in McAllister's Millennium Bug. — **13**

THE CASINO

The Casino, a local landmark, started as a 17th century cottage on the Talbot estate. It is probably what is described in Dalton's History of County Dublin as "Mrs. Clare's pretty cottage". In the early 19th century, an extensive addition was built comprising two large reception rooms and an intervening round hall and entrance hall. Later in the century the Byrne family were the tenants and in 1888 John Dickie moved from Castlebellingham with some of his family to live at the Casino.

Earliest pictures of the house around 1900 show white-washed walls and no ivy but otherwise a similar appearance to the present, although one of the windows seen from the Dublin Road is part of a renovation in 1975 when much of the internal woodwork and plaster was restored and the kitchen and bathrooms re-designed.

Considering the proportions of the house it is perhaps surprising that it never had more than four bedrooms.

In 1901 the house was used as a model for the Irish pavilion at the Glasgow Exhibition.

More recently it was again in the news with the sad departure of the donkeys that were so much a part of the Casino scene for twenty years and a vivid memory for generations of Malahide's children.

While the property has now passed out of the Dickie-Kirker family after five generations and over one hundred years, the building and its vista from the road will be permanently preserved and should continue to give pleasure to all who pass by.

The Casino – **1**

The main entrance door, intervening hall and entrance hall. – **1**

Mrs. Elizabeth Kirker enjoying a quiet read in the sitting room. — **1**

Previous owners, the Byrnes and Dickies had etched their names on the windows of the sitting room. The Kirkers have added their names and that of their son to the window. — **1**

Relaxing in the porch, a conservatory type room at the front of the house, are Dr. John and Elizabeth Kirker, who will shortly vacate the Casino as owners, thus ending a long family association of five generations with the house. – **1**

Enjoy the delights of the natural history of Malahide Castle. – 15

Marina View. — **13**

The new Cruzzo's Restaurant at Malahide Marina. — **14**

The moorings at the Marina. — **10**

Local fisherman, Paul Clancy. — **11**

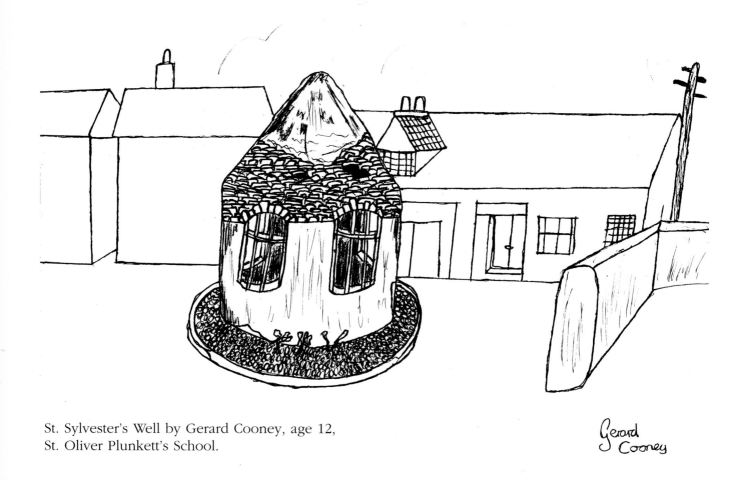

St. Sylvester's Well by Gerard Cooney, age 12,
St. Oliver Plunkett's School.

MALAHIDE

Malahide is the place to be.
You can go to the shops or swim in the sea.
There's so many places to go to –
The Castle, the Well, Hick's Tower, Casino.
There's amazing places to eat,
Fun things to do,
So come along and enjoy yourselves
There's so much in store for you.

By Sarah Wrigley, 4th Class, Pope John Paul II School.

Built in 1956 "The Red School", St. Sylvester's Junior School, caters for pupils from Junior Infants to First Class. — **1**

Lollipop Lady, Frieda Markey, shepherds Rebecca and Alannah Griffin, Brian and Niamh Shalloe, Sean and Elaine Mulcahy across to school. — **1**

Mothers and children arrive at school. — **1**

Memorial at St. Andrew's Graveyard to Nathaniel Hone (1831 – 1917), the famous Malahide painter. In 1892, he was the first Captain of Malahide Golf Club. – 3

On their way to a fourball at the new Malahide Golf Club are: Dr. Peadar Kearns, Michael Dwyer, Tom Kilraine and Denis Hatch. – 12

Memorial window in the Presbyterian Church, donated by Dermot Dickie to honour his parents. – **2**

A view of the Catholic St. Sylvester's Church from the window of the Presbyterian Church. – **2**

"The mass is ended. Go in peace". Eileen Harmon, Maisie D'Arcy and Sheila Toft, enjoy a chat after morning mass. – **1**

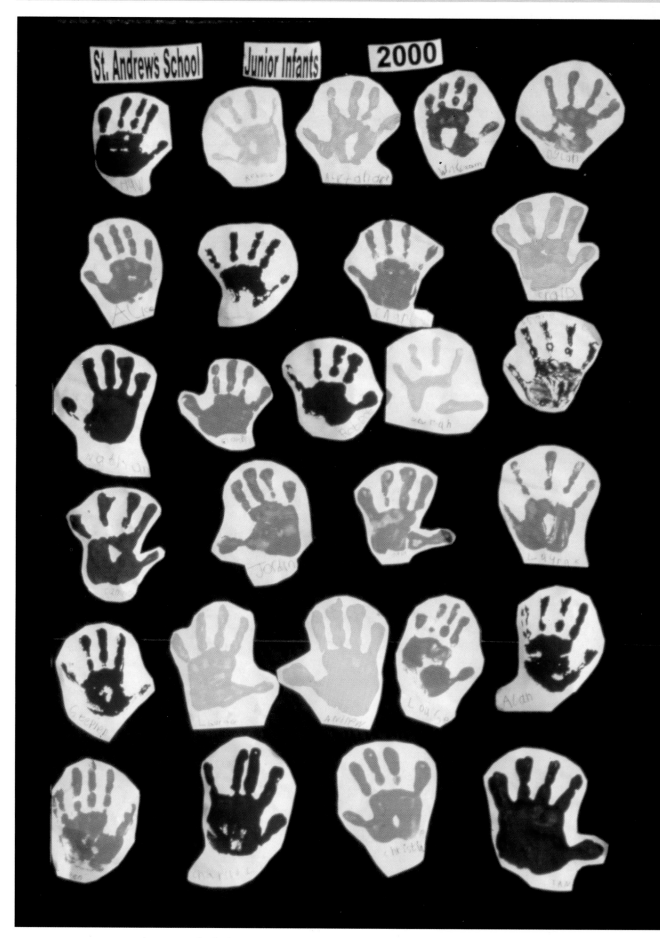

Handprints of all the Junior Infant Class of 2000 at St. Andrew's School. — 9

Junior Infants at play in St. Andrew's School with teacher, Ruth Sloan. — 9

Children from 17 different nations attend St. Andrew's School: Wales, Germany, Japan, Sri Lanka, Ireland, Pakistan, Nigeria, England, Scotland, Romania, France, U.S.A., Australia, Sweden, South Africa, Spain, Chile. — 9

Boatman and ferryman, Billy Hatch, who looks after the moorings in Malahide. — 7

St. Sylvester's Well, in Old Street, is believed to be a natural spring, possibly dating back to prehistoric times. Public baptisms were held here, as was a pattern on August 15th each year. Tradition has it that if you walk around the Well seven times, reciting specific prayers, your requests will be answered. — 7

DUFFY'S OF MALAHIDE

The Main Bar – a blend of South American pine and oak is used extensively throughout the interior to give a warm welcoming feeling. – **1**

Malahide operated the earliest "tide-mills" in Ireland and later became famous as a coal importing port. The coal boats had always to be unloaded on the tide, which meant irregular working hours. It was thirsty work and was particularly inconvenient in the early morning, when the local village tavern was closed. Therefore, a special licensing dispensation was granted, so that the workers could avail of a drink, when the work was completed.

It was not uncommon, therefore, to find the local tavern of Parkinson's busy and alive with the sounds of laughter and merriment from early morning.

That same tavern, which was an essential part of Malahide's social history, additionally operated as a community morgue, grocery store and popular "bona-fide" house.

Today, that historic past is perpetuated and surpassed in "Duffy's of Malahide".

"The Marquee" area is a conservatory, which is adorned by a full wall mural of the beach in Malahide. – **1**

PLENTY OF LEISURE
TIME IN MALAHIDE:

fly your kite – **15**

go canoeing with the Sea Scouts – **4**

have a day out at Low Rock – **11**

or just take a Sunday morning cycle with the children, like Brian and Mona Glenn. – **11**

Eileen Dixon-Jackson, Midge Dunlop and Joy Breivik take time out for a chat and a snack. – 23

Ice-cream time for Alister, Patrick and Andrew. – 23

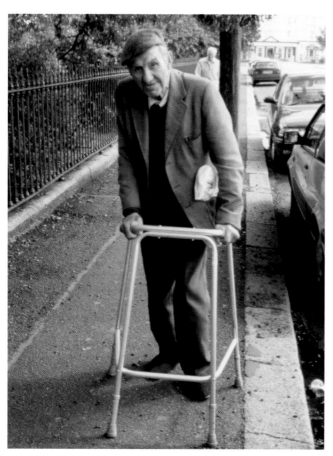

Johnny McGann. – **11**

Mr. McAuley. – **11**

Vincent Markey with his four-legged friend. – **11**

Austin – head-barman at Duffy's. – **11**

Vera Hickey and daughter, Cindy. Vera is a well-known North County Dublin dog handler, breeder and trainer. – 11

Guys of The Eastern Bay (North) Swimming Club, with friends from the Aer Lingus and Viking Clubs. They meet each Sunday morning all year round at High Rock.– 11

Mick Costello, one of the few remaining craftsmen, who make lead letters when inscribing headstones. — 9

Bob Turner, sexton of St. Andrew's collects the grass clippings from St. Andrew's graveyard. Up to a few months ago, Bob used to bring the grass down to Noel Dunne for his cows in New Street. The cows are gone now. — 9

St. Oliver Plunkett's Principal, Tony Healy, with the school's youngest boy, Eoin Fedigan, and the youngest girl, Kristina Murphy, placing organic waste in the composting bin for recycling. — 7

St. Oliver Plunkett's Sixth class pupils preparing items for a time capsule, which will be opened again in the year 2100. — 7

Castle View Montessori School, run by Tina Bossonet. — 7

Litter-conscious pupils cleaning up at St. Oliver Plunkett's School. — 7

The Talbot Family Crest. "Forte et Fidele" - Brave and Faithful. — **14**

Castle by Vicky Connolly, 6th Class, St. Oliver Plunkett's School

MALAHIDE

Welcome to Malahide, in which I have lots of pride.
Malahide is the place to be with lots of things to do and see.
You could even go to the shops and buy a big ice-pop.
Visit the castle; it's not too much hassle.
Or go to the beach, it's not out of reach.
I love playing in the park when it's not too dark.
So come on down to our lovely town.

By Niall McCarthy, 4th Class, Pope John Paul II School.

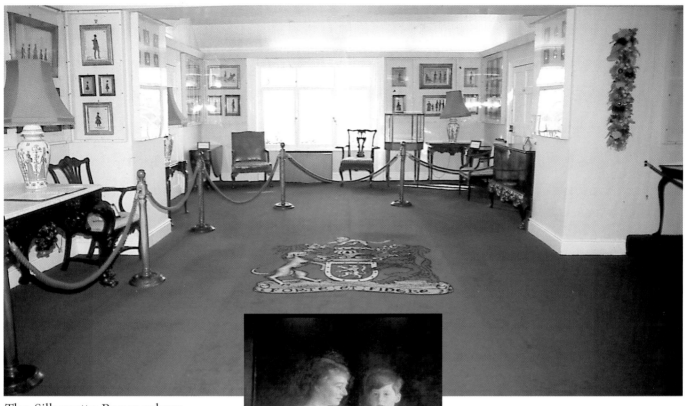

The Silhouette Room where the crest is to be found on the carpet. The silhouettes form the largest such collection in Ireland. – **14**

A painting in the castle portrays Lady Eva, the mother, Lord Milo and Lady Rose Talbot, who is the last remaining Talbot, currently living on the Malahide Estate in Tasmania and who still returns to Dublin once a year. – **14**

The 16th Century remains of Maud Plunkett, who was
".......................in one morning tide,
A wife and a widow, a maid and a bride". – **3**

View of the turrets from inside the castle. – **14**

TDM or Talbot de Malahide on the labourers' cottages built in 1870. **– 12**

Bobby and Maureen Nugent, whose family have lived in a TDM cottage for three generations. **– 17**

Pegram's Thatched Cottage, Sea Road was built in 1870 and would have been originally used by Malahide Castle Estate and lived in by families engaged in farming and fishing locally. **– 12**

Reflections — **7**

Rowboat reflections. — **15**

A lady performs "Tai Chi" on the beach near Robbs Wall. — **7**

THE
MEDICAL HALL

THE MEDICAL HALL

There has been a pharmacy at 1a Church Road since 1972, when it was opened by Sean Moran. Following Mr. Moran's death in 1974, the late Paddy Quinn became the proprietor. He had a long and successful career, and made a number of significant contributions to the spirit of the community of Malahide through his membership of local associations. He was among the first to return to the traditional style of shopfront that contributes so much to the charm of Malahide. Shortly after Aideen Murphy took over the pharmacy in 1995, the interior was refurbished in a style that was consistent with the traditional shopfront. The agreeable and obliging members of staff, Teresa Hammond and Mary Mackey have been familiar figures in the community for many years. This contributes to the blend of up-to-date products, information and advice along with the warm personal touch, which is valued by their customers.

THE CARMELITES OF MALAHIDE

The Carmelites of St. Joseph's Monastery, Seapark, are a community of women dedicated to the contemplative life. Life revolves around times of prayer, mass and spiritual reading. At other times an atmosphere of silence pervades the monastery. Except for two recreation periods, the sisters keep silence, speaking only when necessary about their work. – **1**

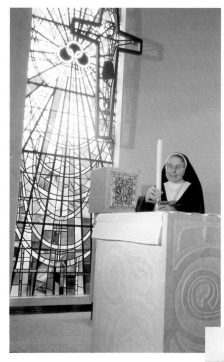

The sisters are vegetarians, keeping to a simple, wholesome and healthy diet.

Work, particularly manual work, has always characterised the contemplative community. To provide variety of work, tasks are often done in rotation. As well as the ordinary daily tasks, the Carmels also run a few "industries": candles, honey and cards are produced and sold locally. Vestments are made and sold nationwide.

Twice a day the sisters come together to talk and relax. The newspaper is available a few times a week. They do not have television. **– 1**

Malahide train station, platform 1. The railway came to Malahide in 1844. – **11**

Station Master, John Kerley. – **22**

The original signal box still stands at the station. – **14**

Aoife, Michael, Caitríona and Sorcha Crosse are taught violin lessons by Dorothy Conaghan in her home. — **1**

New Street vista. — **20**

Colourful shopfronts at the corner
of Main Street and Old Street. — **11**

The arched entrance to
Malahide Marina. — **14**

Jungle Flowers, winners of Best
Shop Front of the Year. Outside is
Patricia Hess with Deborah and
Ruth Owens. — **23**

Who's for tennis? Hélene McCullen, Helen Duggan, Bernie Morris, Anne Murphy, Irene Reilly, Pauline Sorohan, Geraldine Byrne, Liz Roche, and Una Farrell. — **3**

Coaching session at Malahide Tennis and Croquet Club. — **3**

Starting early with a helping hand from Dad is Irene Drew at the tennis courts at Malahide Demesne. — **23**

Malahide United Nippers League. Over 100 nippers are trained here every week. — **12**

Katie Bushe, aged 14, is a 2nd Year student in Malahide Community School. Katie has been selected as a member of a six person gymnastic team to represent Ireland in the European Special Olympic Games in Groningen, Holland, in May, 2000. — **11**

Irish dancer, Maria Gorman. — **11**

Gardaí Gerard Tighe and Peter Kenny setting out on their patrol. – 23

Sinéad Morris selling daffodils to raise funds for the Hospice Foundation. – 17

Watch out when she's about! The traffic warden tries to sort out some of the traffic problems. – 12

Busker, Martin Grogan. – 11

FOCUS ON RELIGIOUS PERSONNEL SERVING IN THE PARISH

Fr. Brennan, P.P. and Fr. Finnerty, C.C., of the Yellow Walls Parish, which was formed out of the Malahide Parish of St. Sylvester. — **1**

Moderator designate of the Presbyterian Church in Ireland, Rev. Dr. Trevor Morrow, addressing the combined congregations of Howth and Malahide in the Presbyterian Church in Malahide. — **2**

Sister Elizabeth Dunne of the Sisters of Marie Reparatrice. The sisters arrived in Malahide in 1994 and are involved in retreats, spiritual direction and parish ministry. — **12**

Sisters Clare and Margaret of the Sisters of the Blessed Sacrament in their oratory in Seabury. These sisters are involved in parish work and education. — **1**

Canon Brady, Rev. Norman Gamble, Fr. Randles and Fr. Young. — **9**

St. Sylvester's Church

by Anna Howard

Artwork by Anna Howard

The beautiful serene interior of the Church of the Sacred Heart,
Yellow Walls. — **21**

GIBNEY'S

The present licence of Gibney's can be traced back to 1845 but for almost a century beforehand this pub had been one of the treasured custodians of the Dublin licensed heritage, sharing a link with the Talbots, through whom the pub came to prominence in

the 1740's as the famous "Golden Lion Inn". During that period, Malahide was famous for its green finned oysters, cotton and silk industries, saltworks and coal yard. At that time Colonel Talbot granted permission for an inn on his lands near the village green, which was known locally as Theatreland, because of its accommodation of visiting circuses and strolling players who spread their tents there.

In 1937, the Gibney family arrived here to what was essentially a "spit and sawdust pub", with a backyard that contained an apple garden and a pungent smelling piggery.

Today, Gibney's receives plaudits for its unspoilt, natural and preserved image. It is a traditional pub which has embraced the modern approach. You can order a pint at the bar or order it on the internet at www.gibneys.com There you will also find corporate gifts, hampers and a wine shop.

Jennifer Ugwaka, Seabury. — **18**

Béibhínn Sheridan-Sii. — **5**

Donald Ryan delivering coal. – 11

David Carroll, cabinet maker and restorer of antique furniture. – 1

Gerry Diem of Malahide Pottery. – 4

John Heron making a cappuccino at Coastal Coffee shop. – 13

"Lookalikes" : Ten sets of twins and one of triplets attended St. Oliver Plunkett's School this year. They are pictured with some of the 2000 daffodils planted for the Millennium by the pupils and teachers. Back row: Nicky & Carl O'Flanagan, Rachel & Rebecca Horgan, Fionn & Aaron Carney, Elizabeth & Eoin Melvin, Fiona & Aisling Kennedy, Shane & Sinéad O'Callaghan. Front row: Jody & Seána Murphy, Christian & Stefan Gibney, triplets Diarmaid, Orlaith & Colm McCaffrey, Jonathan & Adam Fanning, Aisling & Fiona Lee. – 7

Mrs. Roisín Nugent passing on I.T. skills to her students in St. Oliver Plunkett's School. – 7

Students from St. Oliver Plunkett's School enjoying a humorous play about Cuchulainn during Seachtain na Gaeilge. – 7

The entire complement of junior infants and their teachers attending St. Sylvester's Junior School in March, 2000.

Front Row: S. Clarke, E. Cuddy, C Curtis, P. Fox, N. Gaine, S. Green, K. Haskins, C. McGrath, C. Mullarkey, K. Naughton, K. O'Flynn, C. Quinn, M. Roche, B. Timon, C. Barnes, A. Condren, M. Dowling, A. McKinlay, E. Memon, C. O'Donoghue, J. O'Reilly, K. Scandurra, S. Taaffe, S. Walshe – pupils of Mrs. Dunne.

Second Row: D. Barriscale, J. Cooney, J. D'Arcy, D. Fox, R. Grogan, G. Kelly, D. McCormack, J. McDonnell, R. Murray, E. O'Connell, G. Seales, C. Stuart, C. Synnott, N. Byrne, S. Carter, S. Doyle, C. Foster, A. Halpin, L. Hevey, O. Howard, C. Lynch, A. McLoughlin, S. Meehan, K. Vesselova, L. Whyte – pupils of Ms. McGrath.

Third row: D. Collins, H. Daly, J. Dillon, D. Elebert, C. Ginty, J. Hales, L. Honan, S. McCarry, F. Neary, E. O'Keeffe, S. Roote, D. Shanley, C. Tobin, J. Bohan, A. Brady, H. Breen, M. Burke, A. Byrne, S. Comer, N. Coughlan, K. Dunne, A. Elebert, J. Hunt, S. King, R. Lennon, S. Ryan – pupils of Ms. Mooney.

Fourth Row: G. Blain, M. Connellan, A. Connolly, I. Donnelly, D. Feenan, E. Foley, G. Gaffney, K. Gaynor, P. O'Connor, F. O'Neill, A. O'Reilly, M. Palminteri, S. Palminteri, D. Robinson, J. Storey, C. Tormay, G. Young, N. Barber, C. Burke, J. Dowling, M. Fox, A. Griffin, R. Grogan, D. Lynch, R. Lynch, O. McCabe, D. McCarthy, N. Shaloe – pupils of Mrs. Kelly.

At the back: Teachers, Ms. Mooney, Mrs. Kelly, Mrs. Dunne and Ms. McGrath with the Principal, Mrs. K. Murphy. – 1

Gwen O'Connor trains the under-age hockey teams every Sunday. — **1**

"In the thick of it" at Malahide Rugby Club. — **24**

Martin Barnes leaps high above his opponents from St.Brigid's, while 'George' Cloonan and Declan Byrne await the outcome. — **1**

The Under 8 Malahide United soccer team. 39 such teams are catered for by the club. — **1**

Christina Cotter teaching the tin whistle to the children. – **11**

Children from the Busy Bodies Montessori School. – **3**

Mrs. McKiernan. — 11

A group of students from China in Malahide to learn English. — **24**

Some of our European neighbours living and working in Malahide: Florence Hervo (French), Oliver Binachadler (Swiss), Sebastian Schaffer (German), Patrizia Serra (Italian), Axelle Franc (French), Maresa Barrera (Spanish). — **13**

Sarah Donaldson of Fragrance Boutique,
Malahide. – **4**

Kevin Byrne, Fingal Sailing Club. – **11**

Paul O'Rourke, upholsterer. – **11**

Norman Lambe locking up the Library. — **11**

Michael O'Dwyer at the Cottage Museum, Malahide Demesne. He holds a framed citation to a member of the clergy. The Museum was set up by the Historical Society. — **1**

TONY BYRNE MALAHIDE MENSWEAR

Tony Byrne Malahide Menswear is situated at the very heart of Malahide, in what is locally known as The Diamond. The building, in bygone days, served as the local RIC barracks. — 7

Tony Byrne

The final decade of the last century saw a major change in the way some men dress for work and leisure time. Designer quality clothing from GANT USA and LACOSTE are always popular. — 7

"The Best A Man Can Wear"™

Today the average "Baumler" business suit costs £350, teamed with an "Olymp" non-iron shirt at £45 and matching Silk Tie at £25. — 7

Mrs. Dooley's 3rd Class from Pope John Paul II School. — 7

Mrs. McGrath lines up the junior infants to return to class. — 7

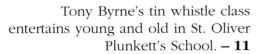

Students waiting in line with their registration forms for their MMR vaccinations. — 7

Tony Byrne's tin whistle class entertains young and old in St. Oliver Plunkett's School. — 11

Robbs Wall by Niall Coughlan, St. Oliver Plunkett's School.

MY HOME TOWN

I WOULD LIKE TO
TELL YOU ALL A TALE
ABOUT WHERE I LIVE
AND WHERE LOTS OF
BOATS SAIL.

MALAHIDE IS ITS NAME
AND NO PLACE ELSE IN
IRELAND IS QUITE THE
SAME.

THE VILLAGE IS A SIGHT
TO SEE
WITH BEAUTIFUL
SHOPS AND BUILDINGS
WHICH ARE LOVED BY ME.

THE PARK, THE BEACH
ARE ALL SPECIAL PLACES
WHERE I LOVE TO
SPEND MANY AN HOUR
PLAYING AND RUNNING RACES.

By Frances Joyce, 4th Class, Pope John Paul II
School.

MALAHIDE
The Greatest Town.

Do you want to see the greatest town,
With shops and parks all round?
Then come on down to our little town –
MALAHIDE!

There's lots of fun things to do,
Like shops, seasides, playgrounds too.
Then stroll on down to our little town –
MALAHIDE!

You can swing on the swings
Or slide on the slides.
So I invite you down to our little town –
MALAHIDE!

So what do you think?
Will you come down?
We all invite you to our little town –
MALAHIDE!

By Aisling Lavelle, 4th Class, Pope John Paul II
School.

Captain Tommy McKeown has crossed the Atlantic 1000 times as an Aer Lingus pilot. In 1979, he was in command of the papal flight from Rome to Dublin. Nowadays, he enjoys a regular jaunt in a much smaller craft around Weston Aerodrome. He can be spotted around Yellow Walls at zero altitude on his bike. "I've been cycling long before I flew", he says. — **10**

David White enjoys himself in the "Optimist Class" at Malahide Yacht Club. — **1**

Lauren and Louise Maguire. — **18**

Seabury children light a candle and say a prayer. — **11**

Stephen O'Rourke and Alan Carroll fishing at Streamstown. — **7**

John Dignam and Joe Hickey with the day's kill. — **11**

Michael Shaw, groundsman, tending the daffodils at Malahide Tennis and Croquet Club. — **3**

Sean Callan, photographer. — **12**

Hick's Tower was originally built in 1805 as a Martello Tower and was converted into a residence by the architect, Frederick Hicks, in 1910. — **24**

Malahide Estuary from the Marina Promenade Walk. — **11**

A tranquil moment. — **6**

Hardy locals who swim each morning all throughout the year: Nan Lindsay, Brendan Forde, Denise Foley, Esther Murray, Jacinta Comiskey, Maureen Tierney and Teresa Murray-Hession. — **11**

Prize winners, Eimear Nugent and Jennifer Murphy. – 11

Students and teachers from Malahide Community School who visited the European Space Centre in French Guiana, South America, in November, 1999. All the students competed in an essay competition, sponsored by the European Space Agency, entitled "A vision of Space and, Astronomy and its benefits for Humanity". The essay written by Jennifer Murphy and Eimear Nugent won the overall prize for Ireland and as a result, 24 students and 3 teachers had an all-expenses paid visit to the ESA launch site where they witnessed the final preparations for the launch of the XMM telescope on board an Arianne 5 Rocket. – 11

Believe it not, on arrival in French Guiana, the group found that the software needed for the aerospace project was actually developed in Malahide!! The firm, CAPTEC, is to the forefront in the development of such software. It also has developed software for the industrial and medical environments. Pictured are Dr. Paul Kermode, Richard Kennedy and son, Ian, of CAPTEC. – 11

Adam Turner parked outside Malahide Castle — **20**

Hanna Spain — **15**

The Head-Warden's house in Malahide Castle. — **2**

St. Sylvester's Hurling teams play their home matches at the castle grounds. — **5**

Malahide and Portmarnock under 12 teams gather for a game at Bridgefield. — **11**

Rugby players at their club grounds. — **24**

Girls' day out at the Castle for Bernie, Helen and Clodagh Murphy. — **1**

Dancing lessons at St. Sylvester's School. — **11**

Gravediggers, John Barry
and Kevin Brown. — **11**

The Craft Shop at
Malahide Castle. — **20**

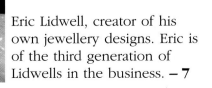

Eric Lidwell, creator of his
own jewellery designs. Eric is
of the third generation of
Lidwells in the business. — **7**

The swans on the Broadmeadow estuary. — **3**

Narcissi at the Castle. — **10**

Poet and writer, Pat Ingoldsby, outside the house where he was "born and bred". – 11

SMYTH'S

"FAMILY & SPORTING IRISH PUB"

This jewel of the Dublin licensed trade has been fulfilling the social needs of North County Dublin for over one hundred years. When Michael Hogan acquired the first license in 1896, this coastal haven of Malahide was but a quiet, unobtrusive sea village, populated by declining numbers of the ascendancy classes and serviced by thriving coalyard and fishing industries.

In the early years this pub operated a 7 a.m. opening licence to accommodate those employed in the coalyards who unloaded their cargoes at high tide. The pub also served as a community morgue and frequently held overnight the bodies of those who drowned or who died in accidents on the Great Northern Railway. In its history this pub has only had three family ownerships: the Hogans, Nolans and the current hosts, the Smyth family, who purchased the premises in 1979. – **1**

"The Marine Lounge" is dedicated to Malahide's historic association with the sea and all forms of navigation. — **1**

"The 19th Hole" is dedicated to the great golfing exploits of our nation. Encased here in oak and glass cabinets you will find all the relevant trivia of Ireland, including the golfing bag carried to victory by local Malahide hero, Philip Walton, at the Ryder Cup. — **1**

Sand dune on Malahide beach. — 3

The craft courtyard at Malahide Castle. — **20**

Early commuter at Malahide Train Station — **20**

Larking in the park, Pat Spain and his daughter, Emma. — 15

John Murtagh taking time out. — 11

Members of the Girls' Brigade. — **9**

Some members of the Young Dublin Symphonia Chamber Orchestra taking a break from rehearsals. — **9**

Alex McAllister chatting with his aunt, Mrs. May McAllister, at her home, La Mancha, where she has lived for 50 years. — **2**

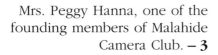

Mrs. Peggy Hanna, one of the founding members of Malahide Camera Club. — **3**

Commuters at the busy station. — **18**

Malahide at the crossroads. — **17**

Keeping fit. — **12**

Jamie Prior with Jodie. — **3**

Vet Wiliam McCartney and Bernie Bushell with two of their patients. — **22**

Mrs. Carole O'Brien, her son, Seán and the Principal of St. Sylvester's Junior School, Mrs. Karina Murphy, have a look at the "Early School Days" project. Mrs. Murphy taught Carole and can be seen in the old photograph in the project. — 7

Joining some members of the school staff are visitors from Finland, Germany and U.K. who came to St. Sylvester's Junior School to learn about Ireland's education system as part of the European Education Network Conference which was held in Malahide. — 7

Gareth Giles imparts his advice to the attentive ears of Niamh Sweeney, Aisling Black, Riona McGrath, Neave O'Clery in the "Mirror Class" at Malahide Yacht Club. – **1**

Jet skiing on a Sunday afternoon. – **24**

Under coxswain, Thomas McLeod, the lifeboat sails up the Malahide estuary from Kinsale. – **24**

Spring in the grounds of the Castle. – **2**

Eithne La Blanc on her way to marry Mr. Flavio Vincente. – **12**

Eric Crampton, proprietor of "The Pottery Shop, Malahide", which opened for business 22 years ago and has become internationally famous for its pottery, china and crystal gifts. — **12**

The ARCH Club is an integrated club for able children and those with special needs. It encourages the children to build up their own circle of friends, independent of their parents. In the frame are: Conor Nolan, Sean Nolan, Patrick Leahy, James Leahy, Helen Nolan, Brian Leahy, Eilis Conaty, Carole Anne Bolger, Hannah McLean, Claudia Smyth, Norina Savage, Gareth Savage, Rene Leahy, Nancy Bolger, Lilly Conaty and Michael Leahy. — **1**

Mary Farrell sets out the best sellers at her bookstore "Village Books". — **1**

101 year-old Mamie Mullally has the unique distinction of having lived in three centuries. — **22**

Mr Maurice McDermott, born and reared in Malahide, is a familiar character to be seen on Back Road. 7

Cricket was first played in Malahide in 1861 and the Club is both one of the oldest and one of the most picturesque in Ireland. Many international matches are played here. — 9

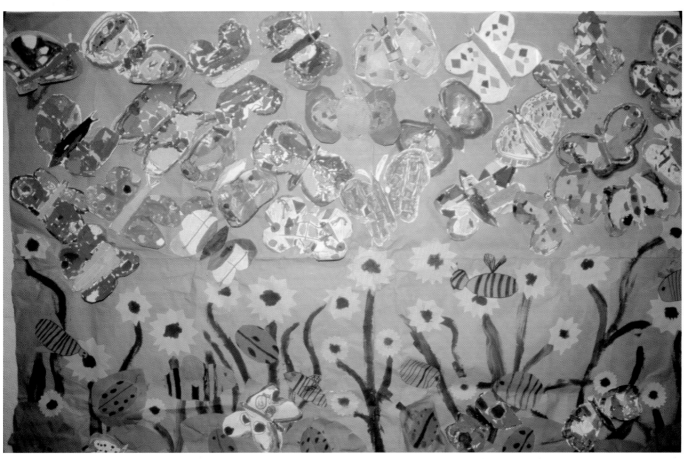

Some of the lovely artwork of "The Red School", St. Sylvester's. — 7

Stephen Aston on the crosstrainer in the new gymnasium at the Grand Hotel. — **1**

Cyclists — **5**

Goal shot. Every Saturday and Sunday are busy at the Castle grounds. — **19**

The band "Celtic Fusion" plays Maud Plunkett's every Sunday: Christie Sheridan, Tony Brennan, Smithy and Tony. – **14**

Dancers "Celtic Rhythm", Aoife Murtagh, Fergal Fay, and Linda Masterson. – **14**

Assistant manager of Maud Plunkett's Hotel, Peter Gavin, with staff members, Gordan Farrell, Keith Lawlor, Mark Byrne, Jennifer Lawlor and Caroline Masterson. – **14**

Gareth Cullen windsurfing on the estuary – **7**

Rainbows over the estuary. – **11**

Valerie Mitten from
Biba's Boutique. — **17**

Volunteer workers, Ann O'Connor and
Eileen Lucy at Oxfam Ireland working
to reduce poverty, distress and suffering
worldwide. — **22**

Gordan McKay and Pat Costigan behind the butcher's counter where Mrs. Weir inspects a prime cut. – **11**

A potter from the Band and Cuffe Pottery operating out of Malahide Castle Craft Courtyard. – **20**

Shoe repairs by Colm Rooney – **11**

Rehearsal time for the Enchiriadis Treis under the direction of Marion Doherty. — 7

Marion is the Malahide Person of the Year, an award from the Chamber of Commerce in recognition of her enormous contribution through music to the life of Malahide. — 7

The winners of the annual Malahide Chamber of Commerce Awards – Palma Cafolla of Jungle Flowers, Best Shop Front; Gary Gilmore of Café Provence, Tidiest Premises; Marion Doherty, Malahide Person of the Year; Eric Crampton, President of the Chamber of Commerce; Breda Gaffney of Paolo Rossi, Most Improved Premises; Pat Caulfield of Shoe-B-Doo, Best Christmas Window. – **1**

Malahide Lions Club: M. D'Arcy, S .McDonagh, F. Keating, F. Higgins, Liz Byrne, M. Ryan, J. McCormack, B. Twamley, P. Douglas, B. O'Byrne, T. Maverley, B. Quinn, B. Maher, T. McCarthy, P. Mullock, P. Dunleavy. – **4**

Garda Cleary at work. Eddie was Malahide Person of the Year in 1999. — **24**

Richard Taaffe — **18**

Nuala Dignam has worked at McAllister's Garage and shop for many years and is frequently spotted on her bike. — **9**

Michael Ingoldsby with his model of the circus which used to camp on Malahide Green. — 11

Dominic Rooney and Paul Roberts installing a new piece of sculpture on Malahide Green. — 7

AIB

YOUR NEEDS ARE CHANGING – SO IS YOUR BANK

As we begin the new Millennium, AIB, Ireland's largest bank, is continuing to evolve to meet the needs of our customers. We have developed a new concept in branch design and merchandising that focuses on a retail-banking environment to suit these needs.

In September 1999, AIB Malahide moved from a sub office in Main Street to a full branch in Church Street to encompass this new design.

At AIB, we recognise the demands that today's lifestyle places on our customers. That is why we have made banking more convenient by extending our opening hours in Malahide on Thursday and Friday evenings and also by opening on Saturdays.

It is important that our customers can talk to us about their financial needs in a comfortable relaxed environment at a time that suits them. For this reason, our financial specialists are available to give advice on mortgages, loans, pensions and investments no matter where your bank account is held.

We have developed a number of convenient methods of banking with AIB to suit changing lifestyles. These include banking over the telephone or the Internet with AIB 24 Hour Telephone Banking and 24hour-online. Our staff in Malahide is on hand to provide demonstrations of these new services to our customers.

Presbyterian Church by Colm Roche of St. Oliver Plunkett's School

MALAHIDE TOWN

Malahide is great fun,
And it has a beach,
Lights are in the harbour,
And they are beautiful.
Hi, we say to newcomers
In school or on our road,
Dining in a restaurant,
Enjoying yourself in Malahide.

Time to see some sites,
Our Malahide Castle is lovely,
With all the beautiful sites you will have to come
Now it's time to say goodbye.

By Aisling O'Brien, 4th Class, Pope John Paul II School.

Irish music in Duffy's every Thursday night: Liam Curran on the fiddle and Maurice Mullen on the flute. — 7

Emer Roche on the fiddle. — 7

Liam Curran. — 1

The Band in full regalia. — **11**

Members of Malahide Pipe Band in practice. — **5**

Alan Kenny, artist. – **18**

Pauline McCurdy enjoying her art class, one of the many night classes available in Malahide Community School as part of its Adult Education Programme. – 7

Malahide Marina insignia. — **10**

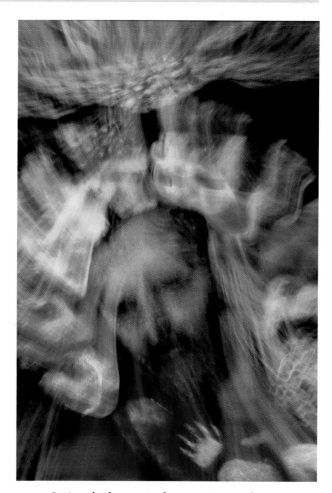

Stained glass window in St. Andrew's
Church — **9**

Colourful faces. — **9**

A grey squirrel in the grounds of Malahide Castle. — **11**

Judith Purdy and Lorcán O'Toole – night revellers. – **13**

Patrick O'Reilly, former boat builder in Malahide from 1972 – 1980, enjoys his drink in Duffy's. – **1**

THE GRAND HOTEL

The entrance to the Grand Hotel. **– 1**

The Grand Hotel was built by James Fagan M.P. in 1835 but its original name was the Royal Hotel. Visitors arrived by stage coach, necessitating the removal of the town's foundation to facilitate their passage.

The Dublin to Drogheda Railway arrived in 1844 and lead to Malahide becoming a holiday centre for Dubliners.

In 1897, the Hotel was purchased by Mr. H. Bethell. At this time the struggle for National freedom was in resurregence. Reflecting this, he decided to change the name to the Grand Hotel.

A Dr. Colohan acquired the Hotel in 1911 and by all accounts he was quite a character. He had the hotel repainted in pink in honour of his favourite drink, pink gin. The Hotel became known far and wide as the "Pink Hotel". He was also a great motor enthusiast, importing the first petrol driven motor car to Ireland in 1897.

During the First World War, airships were based at Malahide Castle and the Grand Hotel was designated as Headquarters for the British Army, should a German invasion take place.

In the 1920s most of the country achieved its freedom and the Hotel was purchased by the Cavana family who operated it for nearly 30 years.

When the 1970s arrived, the Hotel seemed to have seen its best days. However, in 1974 it was purchased by Matthew and Maureen Ryan and an ever expanding investment programme commenced.

Today, the Grand Hotel has surpassed its former glory days and is a leading four star hotel serving, not just Dublin, but the world.

The swimming pool of the new leisure complex in the Grand Hotel. — **1**

The gymnasium in the leisure complex. — **1**

The beautiful old stairs in the foyer of the hotel. — **1**

Evening light on the estuary. — **11**

The crypt beneath St. Sylvester's Church. — **14**

St. Sylvester's R.C. Church by night. — **11**

Teatime for Andrea, Clara, Ciara, Erika and Helen Jones. — **18**

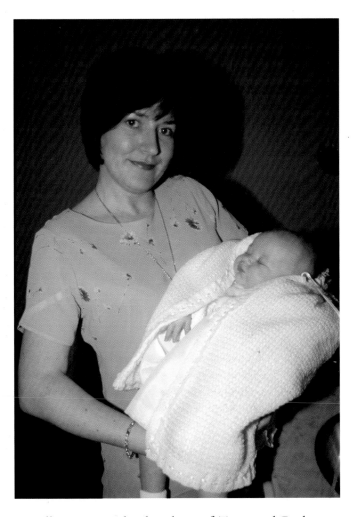

Mollie Kavanagh, daughter of Tom and Barbara, was baptised on 18th March, 2000. — **12**

Kate McSherra and Róisín Anglim ready to dance the night away. — **22**

Some of Malahide's retained firefighters: James McLoughlin, Alan Nangle, Kevin Howard, Paul McEvoy.
In the cab: Tom McLoughlin. — 7

Cub scouts have some fun with the hose. — 7

The fountain on the approach to the Grand Hotel. – 6

Car light trails through the village centre. — **16**

The Village Shop. — **16**

Night falls. — **11**

"I am special" - Part of the Alive - O Programme in St. Sylvester's School. — **7**

Conor Cassin giving a "short back and sides" for IR£4. — **13**

An anchor, originally from a British man o' war sailing ship, now rests at Malahide Marina. — 24

Chef from Cruzzo's Restaurant. — 11

Carmine Mazzole from Angelo's Take Away. — 18

Staff from the Wine Bar, New Street. — 17

Wang, Winnie, Katty, Josephine from Silke's Restaurant. — 18

Night view of yachts in the Marina. — **24**

Train passing over the viaduct which crosses the estuary. — 11

An old tug in the estuary. — **11**

Members of Malahide Camera Club:

Front Row: Harry Reynolds, Gerry Maguire, Helen Hurley, Deirdre Gaffney, Colm Reilly, Judith Purdy, Harry Harrison.

Middle Row: Colette Farrelly, Mervyn Robinson, Robbie Butler, Dave Corbett, Valerie Murphy, Helen McEvoy, Peggy Hanna, Charlie Buckley, Bill Hatch.

Back Row: Jim McManus, Peter Barriscale, Brendan Rooney, Lorcán O'Toole, Joseph O'Hanlon, Therese McGarry.

Absent: Dara Scott, John FitzPatrick. – 24

In this book, the photographers have been allocated numbers. If you wish to identify the photographer, check the number which accompanies the photograph.

1: Harry Reynolds	2: Peggy Hanna	3: Deirdre Gaffney
4: Charlie Buckley	5: Joseph O'Hanlon	6: Dara Scott
7: Peter Barriscale	8: John FitzPatrick	9: Mervyn Robinson
10: Colette Farrelly	11: Bill Hatch	12: Brendan Rooney
13: Lorcán O'Toole	14: Dave Corbett	15: Colm Reilly
16: Therese McGarry	17: Helen McEvoy	18: Gerry Maguire
19: Helen Hurley	20: Judith Purdy	21: Jim McManus
22: Valerie Murphy	23: Robbie Butler	24: Harry Harrison